The Papercut Keeper

Caryssa Ozuna

The Papercut Keeper © 2023 Caryssa Ozuna

All rights reserved.

No part of this publication may be reproduced, stored in a retrieval system, or transmitted, in any form or by any means, electronic, mechanical, photocopying, recording or otherwise, without the prior written permission of the presenters.

Caryssa Ozuna asserts the moral right to be identified as author of this work.

Presentation by *BookLeaf Publishing*

Web: www.bookleafpub.com

E-mail: info@bookleafpub.com

ISBN: 9789357748599

First edition 2023

My beloved sisters and supportive partner.
Without I would never have made it this far.
Oh, and my precious cat, Yami of course.

The Keeper

Broken promises and empty words
Wants and needs left unheard
Far too heavy to be kept inside
The library is where they hide
Script put to paper
Love shown through labor
The lonely word hides from the reaper
Protected by the valiant keeper
Pledging their life to protect this hall
Oath fulfilled until they fall

Sui

I sculpted her
Sired through my hands
Every snip and bend calculated
Formulating a worthy guardian
With folds for joints
And paper for skin
Exhaled life into her
Gave her a purpose

Protect their stories
Make a garden of these weeds

Aster

They made me a picture

Filled it with shapes and colors
Gave sound to the scribbles
Scents to the doodles

I adored it

Unaware that cloaked by the hues
Hid the sketch of humanity
Threatening to rip the splendor to shreds

A personal paradise
Existing just for now

Savor the sweetness
Enveloping your tongue
As it melts away
The taste lingering
Until it's gone

Iris

I was afraid of the dark
So you kept the light on

You were allergic to peaches
So I gave you apples

I didn't want to go home
So yours became mine

You needed a shoulder
So I carried you

We were alone
So we had each other

Daylily

5

Cats learn by mirroring behavior
An unsocialized cat
Struggles to keep up

So I watched

You pick at your stomach and frown
Choking down leaves and water
Appeasing an immovable scale

Hear the words you echo to yourself
Waste away beneath your sheets
As the tears wash your face

I accept the love you receive
And mirror your smile

While I wonder what I did to hurt you

Hyacinth

Pick me up
Throw me in a box
Misspell the label and shove it in a corner
As I start to gather dust
And daylight fades
Toss in one more
Wait a few years
Then another
Forget us in the corner
To create our own secret language
Ignoring the rust

Gloxinia

Tell me about your day

Every detail

Let me be there beside you

I want to hang on to the words
Dangling from the edge of it

While you lull me into quiet
The racket ceases
And I embrace the silence

The calm I can only find
As I listen and trace
The twist of your curls
Relishing your melody

Jonquil

I match your breaths

Inhale
Exhale
Desperate to draw in any piece of you

And if you gasped for air
I would empty my lungs into yours
Suffocated by my own devotion

Grateful for a death
That served you

Calla

There is a stranger
A disgusting revolting thing

Staring back at me

I try to be polite
But words escape me
Not a nice thing to be said

I want to split her apart
Shuck her flesh from her bones
Cut the hair from her head
Claw the mistakes from her body
Leaving only the studs
To be rebuilt from the ground up

If I could not feel pain
I'd be surrounded by myself in pieces

Hellebore

Why settle for a snack
When you can have a feast

Gorgeous pies
Stunning roasts
Beautiful wines
Charming puddings
Elegant breads
Intelligent sweets
Exquisite sides

Everything and anything
Laid out in a menu

The world is your buffet
Gorge yourself
I'm a glutton for pain

Begonia

The spark took quickly
Embracing the parched paper

A fault overlooked
Until the smoke burned our throats

Hydrangea

Tell me again
How did it happen

When did everything
Become nothing

You healed my fractures
Only to shatter me again

I wish you had just left me
With the damage of my own volition

Instead of breaking off a piece for yourself
When I had finally been whole

Peony

13

The church bells never sang for her
But she loved their melody
The umbilical restraint
Joining the union of two children

As alike as drugs and prayer

But the show must go on

And on
And on
And on

Until the stage collapses

Forsythia

14

The shadows in the hall
Dance around the brilliant light
Of the terrible flame

Marigold

15

Let me leave this world
But save you from the hurt

My body nourish you as I decay
My corpse a nursery

Hair becomes cabbage
Bone become carrots

Teeth, sweet berries
Eyes, oranges

Consume all of me until I am gone
Do me this one mercy

So I may finally rest in peace

Poppy

I am a sock

Holey and shrunk
Stuck behind the drum
From well-loved to forgotten

A ceaseless cycle

Wash, rinse, repeat

Fir

The doll did what she could
But what is paper to fire

There is only so much
Before you have to run

As the heat of the flames lick at your skin
And derma curls away from your body

Amaryllis

Tell me a story
Fill it with all your ugly truths
Pour out your heart
Embrace the sentiments

I don't need structure or syntax
Let me feel with you
As we shoulder these words
Together

Empty yourself onto me
Your eager chalice

Cyclamen

Find me one soul
Who has never been hurt?

And you'll have found a soul unlived

Rejoice in the pain
For the next joy will be all the sweeter

If sorrow is the price
For the immeasurable bliss

I shall pay it tenfold

As I wait for the next delight
Mending my cracks with gold

Finis Sui

Paper legs can't run very fast or far
Certainly not as nimble as flames

Her knees turned to ash
And she collapses before the threshold

Fingers outreached
Grasping at a lost salvation

Born in this library
Ending in it as well

The only solace being
That the stories were kept safe

Now and Forever
In her
In you

The Kept

21

Broken promises and empty words
Wants and needs left unheard
Far too heavy to be kept inside
So the library is where they hide
Script put to paper
Love shown through labor
The lonely word hides from the reaper
Protected by the valiant keeper
She kept her oath till death
Preserving their story with her last breath

www.ingramcontent.com/pod-product-compliance
Lightning Source LLC
La Vergne TN
LVHW050509210726

843509LV00015BA/3219